Also written by the author

The Dragonslayers Club

What if there was a horrible fire-breathing "drug dragon" destroying you and your familyl? What if there was something you could do to help yourself- and other kids whose lives have been torn apart by this dragon? The Dragonslayers Club is a fact-based story about a special club where some students found out they were not alone,

The Little House Who Didn't Lose Hope
Second Edition

This story is a heartwarming present-day parable for anyone of any age who needs to be inspired and encouraged- especially those who have felt abandoned, bullied, or hopeless. It also addresses the negative consequences and effects that drug use can have on a family.

Zeeko

Zeeko is a poignant tale of a sweet, fun-loving bunny who decides to go down a dangerous path, which leads him to a forbidden garden. Themes are the dangers of drugs; impact on the individual and their family; collaboration; and loving intervention.

Nita Brady has done it again.
Real – and compelling – taking you on a journey that many of us have gone through, and our children go through today. I loved it. A must read for parents and children alike. It's easy to forget the journey that our young people go through. Nita has a remarkable gift at infusing life lessons in an attractive story filled with struggle, grief, loss, love, connection, addiction, peer pressure, triumph, and near death experiences. All of which is spoken in a language that our young people can understand and relate to.

As I read I wondered what my journey would have been like if I would have had access to this book when I was enduring the difficulty of my teenage years.
Thank you, Nita, for saving our children.

Michael Baldwin CEO MBS Consultants
Founder & Director of Legacy Alliance Outreach

Jenny's Journey is a beautifully written story of making beauty out of ashes. Loss, and the adjustments of life after loss, can be difficult for anyone of any age. Jenny's story is relatable to most: loneliness, anger, and the difficulty of having to navigate through major life adjustments—yet providing the message of hope, love, and restoration. This book will be a great tool for both kids and adults, regardless of age, as author Nita Brady creatively illustrates Jenny's difficulties, wrapped in a simple message of God's love.

Cristina Green, Director of Youth Services
Stanislaus County Gospel Mission

Like an artist with a brush, Nita beautifully paints a story that takes you to "Smalltown USA," and highlights the temptations and challenges a young orphaned girl named Jenny faces as she tries to fit in.

This could be the story of any teenage child today as they are forced with decisions that can affect the rest of their lives.

Peer pressure is very real, and what I love about this book is that not only does it portray the aspects of negative peer pressure, but also the rewards for making right decisions. I believe this book will be a wonderful and imaginative tool that can actually help a young person face life choices.

Lisa Frazier
Recovery Pastor, Celebration Center

Jenny's journey is a story of a young girl's tragic loss—and unexpected gain. Out of loneliness and the desire to be accepted, Jenny makes a choice which takes her through an event which is filled with pain and sorrow, but ends in unexpected faith, hope, and love. This beautifully written story includes practical suggestions and solutions to key issues, and encourages additional group discussion. It is another great and inspiring book by Nita Brady.

Lynn Goldstein
Executive Director for Friends Outside (Retired)

Jenny's Journey

∽

Nita Brady

Jenny's Journey

Copyright © 2021
Nita Brady

All rights reserved.
This publication may not be reproduced, stored in a retrieval system, or transmitted in any form, recording, mechanical, electronic, or photocopy, without written permission of the author. The only exception is brief quotations used in book reviews.

Comments - author email:
Nitab.sos@gmail.com

website: www.familyinmatesupport.com

Cover: Ruth McKinsey

ISBN:
Paper Back   978-1-950768-33-2
Hard Cover   978-1-950768-34-9

Prose Press/WingMan Books, is a division of
Addiction Resource Systems, Inc..

Prose Press
Pawleys Island, SC
prosencons@live.com

Dedicated to educating children of all ages
about the hazards of addiction.

1
A Day to Remember

Jenny slowly opens her eyes and watches the morning rays streaming through her bedroom window. Her bedroom. She still can't get used to the idea that this strange room is her bedroom. Hard to believe it's been a year. She is well aware this is a significant day—the anniversary of an event that turned her life, her world, upside down. She sighs as she slowly gets up, goes to the window, and looks outside. Although what she sees are beautiful, lush green rolling hills, tall leafy trees, and flowers bursting with color everywhere, it still feels foreign to her, even after a year. The current sounds she hears are also quite different from the sounds from her former life. Gone are the sounds of a busy city waking up, the sounds of cars, trucks, and neighbors in the surrounding apartments. She hears a rooster crowing, birds singing, dogs barking, and cows mooing in the neighboring field. Yep, this is one Podunk town she now lives in.

She closes her eyes and pictures her bedroom in the apartment she had lived in with her parents and her little brother Jake. A tear rolls down her cheek as their faces appear in her mind. How she misses them! Yes, even Jake who was always so annoying. She fiercely wipes the tear away, shakes her head, and sighs again.

She looks around this room that had been brightly painted and made to look cheery before she got here. She brought just a few things with her, the framed pictures on this small bedside table, and a few cherished items. Her eyes wander around the room then settle on her most prized possession: something standing tall and proud in the middle of her shelf. She sees her colored drawings and paintings propped up against her wall, waiting to be hung up. She has done a lot more drawing and painting this past year, mostly of horses and dogs, her two favorite animals. Her eyes rest on one that makes her smile. Pogo. One of the family dogs. They have four. He's what they call a puggle, half beagle, half pug. From the moment she met him he'd been friendlier than all the others, worming his way into her heart.

A soft knock on her door, and a voice she is still getting used to, calls her name gently from the other side. "Jenny? Jenny, dear, are you awake?" She also hears the sound of running feet and little giggles being hushed.

Jenny swallows the lump in her throat, and answers

her aunt. "Yes Aunt Bunnie, I'm up. I'll be out in a minute. Just got to get dressed." Guess there's no choice now, she thinks, got to get up.

"OK, dear, take your time. We've got a little surprise for you," her aunt answers.

As Jenny walks over to her dresser drawers, her eyes look up to the shelf above it again, as always. There it is, her beloved white horse statue, standing tall amongst various trinkets and personal items. She has brought it with her from New York City. Standing stately in the middle of the shelf, it is her favorite. She calls him Champion, which fits him well. He looks like a champion racehorse. Or sometimes she imagines he is the magnificent horse Pegasus, from Greek mythology, even if he doesn't have wings. Since he is pure white with a beautifully flowing mane and tail, it's easy to imagine his wings. She reaches for him now and clutches him to her chest and sighs deeply. "Oh, Champion, my Champion; it's going to be OK, isn't it?" Jenny knows she is getting too old to imagine Champion is real, can actually hear her and understand her. She closes her eyes and goes to a place she often visits, especially this past year. She and Champion are galloping down the winding dirt roads, the wind in her long dark hair, feeling exhilarated, waiting for that special moment when suddenly his invisible wings appear visible as he propels himself into the air. Up, up, up he takes her as she sees the fields, the trees, and the dirt roads below her. Ah, her Champion has become her Pegasus, and she doesn't have a care of the world! In this place where she and Champion soar above the clouds, there is no bad news. No police officer coming to tell her on her birthday the horrific truth that would change her life forever. The news that a drunk driver hit her family's car head on, as they were making their way to come pick her up from her best friend Monica's house. They had stopped to get her birthday cake and a few more gifts for her. Her horse figurine was one of them, found in the wreckage. In this special place with him flying above the earth, there is no crying, no painful nightmares, no terrible images of the car wreck, as she soars in the air so freely astride her Champion. There is only joy in this place. There is only her and Champion, soaring above the puffy clouds as she laughs, loving the feeling of being one with her magnificent flying steed.

She opens her eyes, her hands still clutching the figurine to her chest. She sighs once again as she kisses his nose and slowly puts him back on the shelf. "See you later, Champion," she whispers. Another memory drifts across her mind as she slowly dresses. Central Park. That's where her father often took her riding. Back before the "dark time." He had promised her that one day he would buy her a real horse. He said they could keep it at a stable in upstate New York, and he would take her to see him every Saturday. Now she will have to be content with daydreaming and vivid imaginings.

Yes, it's time to get up and face the day, because it is a special day, in more than one way. Today is her 13th birthday.

2
The Gift

As Jenny slowly makes her way down the hall to go into the dining room area of her aunt and uncle's home, she thinks about how different they are from her parents. Her aunt and her mother are half sisters, who only met each other later in life. Her aunt, whose name is Bunnie, married a guy named Bubba. Yep. Bunnie and Bubba. Her parents had more normal sounding names, Tom and Nancy. Bunnie and Bubba grew up in North Carolina, so they sound a lot different than her parents, who grew up in New York City. A whole lot different. It's another thing that's hard to get used to around here, everyone talks so…funny. But they all think *she* is the one who talks funny. All of the kids at her school think she sounds funny; some of them even beg her to say certain words or phrases so they can laugh at the way she talks. They made fun of her for saying "yous guys" but what about them? It's "y'all this" and "y'all that" –

even when they were just talking to one person! Gimme a break! They sound ridiculous to her. In a whole year there was only one girl in her seventh grade class who had been nice to her, a shy girl named Anna, who doesn't have any friends either. She never makes fun of the way Jenny talks, and is really sweet. Jenny wishes she could see Anna more often at school, but they have different lunch breaks.

As Jenny rounds the corner to go into the dining room, she hears some giggling, and then her eye catches a cluster of balloons tied to her chair, and sees a birthday cake in the middle of the table. This is definitely different than the way things were when she lived in New York. "In this house," Uncle Bubba practically shouts, "we start the birthday celebration first thing in the morning, Darlin'!" Wow. Cake for breakfast. Yep, things are sure different around here. "Now y'all just come on over and have a seat, Sugar," he continues. There it is again, "Y'all." What, was he talking to her and an imaginary friend? She looks away, rolls her eyes, and sits down. For a moment her mind goes to all the birthday celebrations of her past. Her mom would bring in the pineapple upside down cake after dinner, and her father would put the birthday crown on her head, and call her his birthday princess. Of course, her little brother Jake would always stick his tongue out at her across the table while their parents weren't looking. But today, well, today she is sitting at the breakfast table in what still feels like some strangers' house, with uncle Bubba's voice booming, and Aunt Bunnie all aflutter, as two sets of young eyes stare at her from across the table. The twins. A boy and a girl, both six years old, who don't look very much alike, like most twins do. Aunt Bunnie told her they are fraternal twins, which means they aren't identical. Their names are Bobby and Billie Jean. Well, guess that's better than Bunny and Bubba, she muses. Who names their kid "Bunny"?

Aunt Bunnie breaks through Jenny's thoughts, asking her a question. Jenny looks up at her aunt blankly, so she repeats the question, "Your candles, hon, want to blow them out now? Oh, and don't forget to make a wish, now, you hear…?"

And what was up with them always calling her Hon, Sugar, Dear, and Darlin'? Did they forget she had a name? The only name her parents called her was Jenny, or sometimes they shortened it to Jen. She wanted to roll her eyes again, but then she didn't want to be rude. It was, after all, nice that they remembered her birthday. And cake for breakfast? Who would complain about that!

"Oh, uh, yeah. Sure," she answers, coming back to reality. It wasn't a pineapple upside down cake, and there was no crown, but…it was nice. She closes her eyes and thinks, a wish? What do I wish for? I wish for the impossible... Tears start to fill her eyes, so she blinks them away, takes a deep breath and blows the candles out really hard. If only she could blow away the darkness, the pain, the deep sadness. She doesn't miss the look exchanged between her aunt and uncle. She knows they are concerned, maybe even worried. And she knows they feel sorry for her. She blows so hard all the candles go out all at once, and the twins begin clapping.

"Hey! That means y'all will get your wish!" Bobby shouts, beaming at Jenny, as Billie Jean nods her head enthusiastically in agreement. They both grin at each other like they're hiding some secret.

Jenny sadly imagines her little brother Jake sitting between the twins, sticking his tongue out at her, wrinkling up his nose. Oh, what she would give to see that little face again and hear him teasing her, "Jenny Penny, looks like a Henny!" Because he always said her skinny legs look like chicken legs. Oh, Jake…

Her eyes start to fill again, so Aunt Bunnie suddenly chimes in and says, "Tell you what, why don't we take Jenny outside now to show her the birthday surprise, and then we can come back in and have some cake, sound good?" The twins look at each other, clap their hands over their mouth, and start giggling again, their eyebrows going up and down, their eyes dancing. Well, whatever it is, Jenny muses, these two seem ready to burst, afraid the surprise is going to come shooting out of their mouths! She can't suppress a smile as Uncle Bubba gives them a look, and Aunt Bunnie heads for the back door.

"Well, Bunnie Honey, I think that's a fine idea. Yes, let's do that!" He turns to Jenny. "Come on, Sugar, we got a little surprise out back for you, so y'all come on out."

Jenny slowly gets up from her chair. Surprises could be good, right? But then there's always this pressure. What if she hated the surprise? She would have to smile and pretend she loved it. Oh well. Just get it over with, she thinks.

As they walk outside, Uncle Bubba keeps up his chatter, and the twins keep grinning, like the Cheshire Cat in Alice in Wonderland, and Aunt Bunnie has a kind of sparkle about her eyes. "Now, shut your eyes, Sugar. That's it. Keep 'em closed, no peeking. You don't want to spoil the surprise." Uncle Bubba sure seems to be enjoying this whole surprise thing. She plays along, squeezes her eyes tight, and says, "OK, I won't peek."

She stands there for what seems like an eternity, eyes shut, the twins' giggles floating up to her ears, as she tries to imagine what the surprise could possibly be. Try as she might, she just can't imagine what her aunt and uncle might have gotten for her, and why they had to go outside to give it to her. Oh! I know, she thinks. I'll bet it's a bike. They probably don't like having to make a special trip driving me to the middle school every morning, she reasons. The twins' elementary school was in the opposite direction, so everyone had to get up extra early, to get dropped off at their schools on time. Jenny sighs. Well, a bike would be okay. She just doesn't want to admit she'd never ridden one. In the city, they either walked, drove, took a taxi, took a bus, or took the subway to get places. It would be embarrassing to admit she doesn't know how to ride a bike. No wonder the twins are giggling so much. Finally, Uncle Bubba calls out, "OK, Hon, you can open your eyes now. That's right. Go ahead and open 'em."

When Jenny opens her eyes, she cannot believe what she sees. It is absolutely beyond belief. There before her is the most magnificent horse she has ever seen. And not just any horse. A horse that looks identical in every detail to the figurine on her shelf.

Her hands fly to her mouth. She is speechless. All she can do is whisper, "Champion." Tears immediately spring to her eyes.

"What's that, child? What did y'all say?" Jenny looks from her uncle to her aunt as tears of joy run down her cheeks. "Champion! He looks just like the horse figurine my dad gave me! His name is Champion, he's up on my shelf! How did you know? How did you find a horse just like my Champion?"

"Well now, we had some idea didn't we, Bunnie

Honey?" Bubba winks at his wife. "We knew y'all loved that little thing, the way you was always clinging to it. We knew your daddy give it to you, too. When that Social Worker lady in New York City talked to us about you, she told us you never stopped holding it the minute you heard about... well, you know, the accident." It was the first time either of them had ever mentioned that night, in her presence. "So, me and your Aunt Bunnie decided we'd look and look 'til we found you a real one that looks just like your toy one. We thought maybe it would help, and, you know, make y'all happy."

He stops and looks at his wife whose eyes have also filled with tears. She just nods and whispers to Jenny, "We just didn't know what your little horse's name was. Now we do." Aunt Bunnie smiles as Jenny, for the very first time, throws herself into her aunt and uncle's arms, sobbing and thanking them. Uncle Bubba pats her and grins real wide. "Now go on, Sugar. Go get acquainted with your new Champion. He's been waiting for ya. Oh, and don't worry. I was raised with horses, so I'll be able to teach you all the finer arts of groomin', saddlin', and ridin'."

Jenny slowly approaches her new horse, so beautiful in every way, with his magnificent head, extraordinarily beautiful coat, long flowing mane, and strong muscular body. When she approaches him, softly calling his name, he softly knickers back as if he knows perfectly well who she is and has been waiting for her. On his back is an English saddle, the kind she has learned to ride with. Her uncle helps her mount, as Champion is so tall.

"Now just walk him around a bit, Jenny, Hon, go easy. He'll need to get used to you. But he's a fine steed, and very well mannered."

For the first time since she is presented with this extravagant gift, Jenny notices the twins. They both watch her with their little mouths hanging open, their eyes popping out.

She chuckles and walks her horse around the paddock. The twins suddenly run back into the house yelling "Cake! Cake!" Jenny smiles. She will gladly wait for the cake just a little while longer. Right now, she is enjoying the best birthday gift beyond anything she could have ever dreamed or hoped for. A true dream come true.

3
An Interesting Invitation

The days turn into weeks, and Jenny can often be seen astride her beautiful steed on the country roads. She has gotten to be quite the horsewoman as Champion anticipates her every move, and quickly obeys her commands. Her favorite times are those when he really wants to let loose and run. As she has done so many times in the past with her figurine horse, imagining their flights into the skies, Jenny now imagines the same scene with her flesh and blood horse, her Champion. Galloping with his beautiful white mane and tail flowing, contrasting Jenny's long, beautiful dark hair, they are quite a sight. As Champion runs freely, she laughs and whispers, so no one can hear her, "Take flight, my Champion, take me into the skies!" And she imagines his "invisible wings" becoming visible, as he launches up, up, up into the sky. She can be heard laughing as she continues whispering, "Well done, my sweet Champion, well done! You're even finer than Pegasus!!"

At times like these she forgets, just for a little while, her great loss, the great hole in her heart. But other times, it isn't so easy. Especially walking down the halls of her middle school, alone. Or having to listen to the kids mock and tease her. Now they not only make fun of the way she talks, they also call her "Skinny Horsey Girl"! Jenny really hates it. It also saddens her that she still hasn't made any real friends at school; this concerns her aunt and uncle, as well.

Which is why it comes as such a surprise when one day a couple of the popular girls, eighth graders, approach her. "Hey, Skinny Horsey Girl. We're having a sleepover next Friday at Kerri's house. Want to hang out with us?" Kerri was THE most popular girl in the school. Did they really want her, Jenny, the Outcast, to come to their sleepover? She frowns and shoots back, "My name's not Skinny Horsey Girl, It's Jenny."

The girls look at each other. One of the girls, Courtney, who is almost as popular as Kerri, says insincerely, "Oh, yeah, Jenny, sorry. Anyway, wanna join us?"

Jenny is confused and conflicted. Part of her wants to tell them to take a flying leap, that she could care less about their stupid sleepover. But another part of her really wants to join them. She feels…kind of pleased that they would even ask her. She has never actually been to a sleepover, and she is tired of not having any friends. She is lonely. So, she tells them, "Well, I'm not sure. I'll need to check with my aunt and uncle first."

Courtney eyes Jenny like she's a bug under a microscope. "Ok, well, here's my number. Let me know."

As the girls walk away Jenny doesn't hear their hushed conversation. "So, why in the world did Kerrie want us to invite her? Can you believe the way she talks? She's so…lame. And, this sleepover is only supposed to be for 8th graders!" Courtney's friend, Brittany, hisses.

Courtney replies, "Oh, Kerrie didn't really want to invite her. At all. Her mom is making her. I guess she heard about how Skinny Horsey Girl's family got wiped out in a car crash and felt sorry for her. She told Kerri if she didn't invite her to the sleepover, she couldn't go to the concert next month."

Brittany's eyes fly open. "OMG, not the concert of the year?? No way! OK, now I get it. Well, I hope she's not too lame or too much of a little goody two shoes."

Her friend smirks, "Oh, I think Kerri's got some little surprises up her sleeve. She'll know how to get rid of her."

Brittany smiles a knowing smile, and says, "Oh, now that oughta be interesting…" as they walk off together, laughing.

When Jenny tells her aunt and uncle about the invitation, they listen with interest. They look at each other and Aunt Bunnie says "Well, Jenny, honey, if you want to go, it's fine with us. We know that girl's parents, they're a nice enough family. I think it'll be fun."

Uncle Bubba smiles and says, "Sure, have yourself some fun, Sugar. Isn't that what all the girls like to do? Have them slumber party things? Eat a bunch of snacks, talk about the boys, tell ghost stories, stuff like that?"

Aunt Bunnie smiles. "Well, I don't know about the ghost stories, Bubba, but girls do like to have slumber parties, and just talk about all the things girls like to talk about. It's fine with us if you want to go," she smiles again at Jenny.

After Jenny leaves the room, Bubba leans over and softly says, "It's nice she's finally starting to make some friends, isn't it Bunnie Honey?"

"Well, yes, I've been a little worried about her, Bubba," Bunnie sighs. "I mean, I know she loves the horse and all, but I sense she's still lonely. And the principal at that school told me she sits alone a lot, and some of those kids are still making fun of the way she talks. But I think it's gotten better. At least, I hope so…" Bunnie's forehead wrinkles, a look of concern all over her face.

Bubba sees it and pats her knee. "Well, I'm glad she got invited to that PJ party or whatever you call it. That has to be a good sign, don't you think?"

"Lord, I hope so," Bunnie sighs. "I sure do hope so."

4
The Friday Night Gathering

One thing that is somewhat familiar to Jenny in her new surroundings, and reminds her a little bit of home, is her aunt and uncle's prayers over dinner, and prayers before bedtime. Her parents prayed over meals, and sometimes they talked about God, and went to church once in awhile. But Jenny isn't sure she can believe in something she can't even see, and she almost feels silly, the idea of talking to an invisible God. She tolerates it because she really doesn't have much choice. Not with her parents, and not now, either. It's just how it is.

But her aunt and uncle do something she isn't familiar with. They have something they call "a Bible study prayer group" in their home every Friday night. Sheesh. Every single Friday night. Her parents never did that. Jenny doesn't have any interest in participating in these Friday night meetings. She really isn't on speaking terms with this God, even if He is real. She's actually pretty angry at Him, at this point, for taking her family away. Anyway, it seems to her that her aunt and uncle are a bit more fanatical about these things than her parents ever were. So, Jenny never joins them on these Friday nights for the Bible study prayer group, although she knows she would be welcomed if she ever did. But one thing she has started doing, is opening her door a crack, in order to listen in when their meeting starts—just out of boredom and curiosity, of course. They always start with singing these beautiful, melodic songs. Some are lively, others are slower, more quiet. And this guy always plays his guitar. He's actually quite good. Jenny is always interested in this part, as music is something that calms her soul, and takes her to a good place, just like when she imagines Champion is flying through the sky with her on his back. This particular music always makes her feel especially good, and she finds herself drawn to the sound of the guitar and the singing. She also grows to appreciate some of the lyrics. She listens now to the strumming of the guitar and the voices floating through the air, making their way to her room.

"Sweet Holy Spirit,
Sweet Heavenly Dove;
Stay right here with us,
Filling us with Your love…"

Yes, she has come to tolerate these Friday night meetings, although in the beginning she had resented them, because first of all, she couldn't watch TV. Another reason she would never make an appearance at them is because the last thing she wanted was to have a bunch of strangers asking her questions like, "Well, who do we have here?" "Why do you live here?" "Where are your parents?" "Why do you talk like that?"

No thank you! But staying in her room, listening through the crack in her door is something she starts looking forward to, as Friday night approaches. There's also something about this time that makes her think fondly of her parents back in their apartment, when they prayed together over meals and at Jenny's bed time. When the accident first happened, she was very angry at God, and she didn't want anything to do with Him, or with prayer. But over this past year and a half since her world was turned upside down, her heart has begun to soften as her aunt and uncle pray over her, and as she hears certain things that are said at this Bible study prayer group.

But next Friday, she won't be here, listening through the crack. She'll be at Kerri's house, at the sleepover. Hopefully having a good time and making new friends. When her aunt and uncle told her it was fine for her to go, she had mixed feelings. She still does. She wants to make friends. She wants to be accepted. To belong. And they did invite her, right? Maybe it would be the start of something good. Maybe.

5
The Sleepover

The day of the sleepover finally arrives. Jenny is starting to have second thoughts again as she packs up her backpack. Why in the world did she tell these girls she would come to the sleepover? A couple of times she had caught Kerri staring at her in the lunchroom, then she looked quickly away. That was kind of weird. If Kerri wanted her there, why wouldn't she come up and talk to her? Why would she look away like that when Jenny caught her staring at her? It unsettles her.

Jenny hears a soft knock. She knows it must be her aunt, as she always knocks like that, softly. "Jenny, dear, may I come in?"

"Sure, Aunt Bunnie, come on in. I'm just packing some stuff."

Her aunt comes in and sits on the edge of Jenny's

bed. She looks around the room and sees the few things Jenny has brought with her when she came to stay with them a year and a half ago. Framed pictures of her parents. Another one of her and her little brother. And one of the four of them together at Coney Island. Their smiling faces speak of happy times, family times. Bunnie wishes she'd had more time with Nancy, her half sister. They had only just found each other a few years before the fatal accident, through the Internet. Bunnie looks away and sighs. She still can't really believe that Jenny's whole family was wiped out in an instant by some reckless drunk driver. When Bunnie had found out it was his third offense, and the other two offenses only got him a "slap on the wrist" from the court system, it made her very angry. Maybe if he had gotten stiffer penalties with the last incident, Jenny's family would still be alive. She was glad he was held accountable for this third incident. Still, that would never bring them back. Bunnie sighs again. This isn't lost on Jenny, who has been watching her aunt intently. "I sure miss them, Aunt Bunnie," she says.

Bunnie wipes her eyes, nods, and takes a deep breath. She looks into Jenny's eyes and says, "Hon, I have two things I want to say to you. First off, I am here if you ever want to talk to me. About anything. I'm a pretty good listener, or so I'm told. And secondly, I want to say that I hope you have a good time tonight.

Have fun, Jenny! Enjoy yourself, OK? But... if there is any reason you don't want to stay, no matter how late it is, you call me, okay, hon? I mean it. Uncle Bubba or I will come get you."

Jenny looks at her aunt, who is really such a beautiful woman, inside and out. Jenny has never met anyone so kind in her life, and she marvels at her aunt's insight. Ever since she and uncle Bubba had given her such a wonderful gift for her birthday, she has really begun to trust both of them and feels much more comfortable with them.

"Ok, Aunt Bunnie, I will. Yous guys don't need to worry about me. I'll be fine."

When Jenny's uncle drops her off at Kerri's house, Kerri's mom greets Jenny at the door and waves to Uncle Bubba. "Hey, Bubba, how are y'all doing?"

"Can't complain, Doris, can't complain," he answers, then drives off.

Jenny looks a little nervous, so Kerri's mom welcomes her warmly. "Come on in, hon. All the rest of the girls are already here. They're down in the cave." When Jenny gives her a quizzical look, Kerri's mom laughs and says, "Oh, I forgot y'all haven't been here before. It's what we call our finished basement, it's our rec room. The kids like to spend a lot of time down there."

As they near "the cave", Jenny can hear voices, and

suddenly feels self-conscious as she stands at the door to the rec room. The party looks like it's already in full swing. There are seven or eight girls there, laughing, chatting, munching a large variety of snacks, their sleeping bags and backpacks sprawled all over a large carpeted area. They've got the music going full blast, and a couple of the girls are taking selfies. Jenny sees a dart board, pool table, various size bean bag chairs, couches, and card game tables. Painted in huge letters on one wall are the words, "THE CAVE". When the girls see Kerri's mom standing in the doorway, motioning Kerri to turn the music down, all of the girls stop talking and laughing, and just stare at Jenny, then look at each other. They are all eighth graders. Jenny is the youngest one there, a seventh grader, barely 13. She is small for her age; all these girls look so much older to her!

"Girls, y'all say hey to Kerri's new friend. What's your name again, hon?" As Kerri's mom turns to Jenny, Jenny doesn't miss the eye-roll Kerrie gives to the other girls.

Jenny starts to speak, but finds she's suddenly got a frog in her throat. She clears her throat and tries again. "My name's Jenny."

The girls give a half-hearted, "Hey", and then they begin chatting again, as the music is once again turned up to full blast. Jenny recognizes all of them from their middle school. They are all either cheerleaders or baton-twirlers. All of them are the popular girls, looked up to by everyone. What am I doing here? Jenny thinks for the hundredth time. Why did I decide to come? She decides to just stay as quiet as possible so as not to draw attention and give any of them a chance to ridicule her New York accent. Maybe that would be best. She drops her sleeping bag and backpack near her, gets a plate of snacks, and sits down on one of the bean bag chairs.

She watches as the girls put makeup on, listens to them talk about boys, what they are going to be doing during their summer break, and the upcoming concert they are all attending – all except Jenny. She's never even heard of this dumb country singer. It isn't her style of music. In fact, it's one more thing she dislikes about this area. She sits there, feeling like a fish out of water, and once more wonders why she has agreed to come. One of the girls, Crystal, turns to her, and asks, "So, do y'all have plans for the summer?"

Jenny looks down, "Uh, I dunno. Haven't heard about any plans…" Her New York accent comes through real thick, and Brittany and Courtney glance at each other and look like they're trying hard not to burst out laughing.

Suddenly, a door opens from an adjoining room, and a very good-looking young man walks in. It is

Kerri's 17-year-old brother, Daniel. All of the girls stop talking and just look at him. Kerrie jumps up and whispers something to him. "Yep," he answers her in a low tone. "You're all set." He grins and winks at them, then says, "Y'all have fun." Then he gives them a look Jenny can't interpret.

After he leaves, the girls all look at each other, and start giggling. One of the girls says, "Kerri, your brother is so hot!" All of the other girls laugh and agree, except Jenny. Sure, he's good looking, she thinks. But there is something about him that doesn't sit right with her. She can't put her finger on it, but something about him is off–and what was all that secrecy about? What did his comment "You're all set" mean, anyway?

It is getting late, and Kerri's mom is turning in for the night. She sticks her head in the doorway to the rec room with a drink in her hand and says, "Good night, girls. Y'all keep it down to a low roar, OK? We're all sleeping in tomorrow morning, including me!"

Jenny notices Kerri's mom seems to be slurring her words and wonders about it. She likes Kerri's mom, something about her reminds her of her own mom. She doesn't like it when Kerri rolls her eyes, as she says real loud, "OK, mom. Bye."

After Kerri's mom stumbles down the hall, the girls all notice that the mood has drastically changed. Kerri is sitting with her head down, as Courtney comes to sit next to her, and softly asks, "So, have you heard anything from your daddy yet?"

Kerri's eyes look hard as they begin to fill. She quickly wipes them, and says, "Not a word. He left town with that…that…you know what, and now my mom has started drinking a lot more. Anyways, I don't want to talk about it." She suddenly puts on a big smile and says, "Let's have some fun! Hey, pass me some of those Snickerdoodles, Crystal, ok?"

Well, this is interesting, Jenny thinks. Things aren't as perfect around here as I thought they were. She feels a little sorry for Kerri now but doesn't say anything. She stays quiet, eating snacks.

The girls start talking and laughing about some new boy at school they think is cute, when Kerri suddenly gets up and goes into her bedroom. She comes back in with a bowl full of plastic cellophane bags, each with a colored ribbon around it. Through the cellophane it looks to Jenny like sugar cubes. The girls grin at each other and whisper, "Finally!" They each grab a bag and begin quickly opening them. Jenny can't imagine why they are so excited to be getting sugar cubes. But maybe these were extra special, for some reason.

"Yes, Daniel came through for us, again, girls," Kerri laughs. He told me these are even more powerful than the last ones. We'll be going to our happy place even quicker!" The girls all began to giggle and start popping the cubes into their mouths.

It begins to dawn on Jenny what is going on here. Her package sits unopened in front of her. Kerri looks at her and urges, "Go on, Jenny, don't you want to feel good? Just one of those cubes will take you to a place where you'll feel really great!" The other girls nod and agree.

"Come on. Jenny," Brittney agrees. "Y'all don't want to be an old stick in the mud, right? Come on, don't be a loser. Y'all are part of our group now." The girls smirk and nod their heads.

How Jenny longs to hear those words, that she belongs somewhere. That she is accepted. Liked. And it sounds so good to take something that would make her "feel so great." No painful memories to hurt her, drag her down, or take her to a very dark place. And the bag is full of those cubes…she could just have one now, and the others later…

Something in Jenny stops these thoughts in their tracks. What is she thinking? What would her aunt and uncle do if they knew? How would they feel? And anyway, she doesn't need those sugar cubes to feel good or "go to a happy place," she has her beautiful Champion. And a family that loves her. And her artwork, her music. But what would her new friends think if she told them she doesn't want to do what they are doing? An idea comes to her.

"You know what, guys, I ate too many chips and salsa and candy already. My stomach doesn't feel too good. Here, I'll just put mine inside my backpack, and have them a little later. She lets them all see her put the cellophane bag inside her backpack so they won't think she's a total loser. She could at least give them the impression that she's going to eat them later.

"Well," Kerri sniffs, "whatever. Suit yourself." She pops one in her mouth and lays back, and all the other girls do the same. As the night wears on Jenny becomes more and more uncomfortable with what she is seeing. These girls are acting weird, saying weird things, and acting strangely. Jenny doesn't like it. She has heard about different drugs from Monica's older sister. Monica was her best friend back in New York City, who she had kept in touch with when she first moved here. But lately, Monica seemed too busy for her, and she rarely returned Jenny's texts or calls. Wonder what Monica would think, she muses, if she could see me now. Monica's older sister has friends who had gotten very addicted to drugs, and she had warned Jenny and Monica about all these different drugs kids were using. Jenny and Monica had sworn they would never take any of those awful drugs. Now here she is in this terrible situation.

Jenny suddenly remembers what her aunt had said. To call her if she wasn't feeling comfortable, no matter how late it was. Well, it was 3am, but she quietly pulls her cell phone out of her backpack and slips into the bathroom to make the call.

"Jenny, dear, is that you? Are y'all all right?" Her aunt's sleepy voice sounds concerned.

Jenny answers softly, "Yes, Aunt Bunnie, it's me. I'm okay, but I really need to leave now; can you come get me? I'm sorry, I know it's so late." Jenny fights back tears.

"Of course, dear, your Uncle Bubba will be right there. Don't you worry one bit."

As she waits, Jenny thinks about how lucky she really is to have people like her aunt and uncle to live with. They aren't her real parents, and they could never take the place of her mom and dad. But they had proven to her over and over how much they care about her, and she is thankful.

She doesn't want the other girls to notice she is leaving, so Jenny very quietly picks up her backpack and sleeping bag. She tiptoes up the steps of the rec room, and makes her way out to the picture window in the living room, so she can watch for her uncle's car. Not that those girls would even notice anyway. They all seem to be completely out of it. She sees her uncle's car and quietly slips out the front door.

"Everything all right, Sugar?" her uncle asks with concern written all over his face, as Jenny throws her stuff in the backseat and climbs into the car.

"I'm okay, Uncle Bubba. But I really don't wanna talk about it right now, if that's all right."

He looks over at her, concerned and sad that she didn't have a good time, like he had hoped. "I understand, Jen. No problem. I'm real glad you called your aunt."

Jen. He had called her Jen for the first time. It's what her dad always called her. She looks out onto the dark countryside and smiles.

6
Bad Choice/Hard Lesson

The ride home is very quiet; Jenny appreciates her uncle's willingness not to question her. When they get home, she turns to her uncle and thanks him for bringing her home. "I'm just going to pop in to see Champion before I head to bed. Is that okay, Uncle Bubba?"

"Sure, Sugar. That's fine. See you in the morning. Your Aunt Bunnie's making your favorite—French toast with hash browns." He grins.

As Jenny walks out to the barn, with Pogo trotting along at her heels, it occurs to her that this is the first time it doesn't bother her that her uncle called her "Sugar." She smiles, and reaches down to pet Pogo. He is her favorite of all of the family dogs. "What are you doing up so late, boy?" she whispers. He looks up at her adoringly, as if to say any time he could be with her was just fine.

She makes her way to Champion's stall. He knickers quietly as she calls his name out softly. "Oh, Champion," she cries gently. "Being with you takes me to a happy place. I don't need those...those things those girls were taking." She drops her backpack on the bench next to his stall and just hugs his neck. She buries her head in his mane and sheds a few tears. She doesn't even know why she's crying, but it feels good to bear her soul to him. She is exhausted because she has been up all night. And it's been stressful. So, she sleepily turns to go, pets Pogo, and heads towards the house.

Jenny sleeps a long time. She can tell when she wakes up that it is late. The household is busy with all kinds of noise: the twins chattering and running, Aunt Bunnie scolding them, Uncle Bubba talking to a friend on the phone. The man always seems to have one volume—LOUD. Jenny laughs to herself, rolls over, and thoughts of the previous night come flooding in. What had she been thinking? What made her think she would ever fit in with girls like that? And if that's what they call fun, well, she didn't want any part of it.

She slowly gets up, gets dressed, and makes her way out to feed Champion. Since she'd slept in so late, she knew he'd be extra hungry! He is always used to eating early. As Jenny walks towards the barn, she can't get this tune out of her head. It just keeps playing over and over. What did they call that? Oh, yes, an "earworm," she laughs. Good way to describe it. It's that song she always hears them sing at the Friday night prayer group. She starts singing it softly to herself, "Sweet Holy Spirit, Sweet Heavenly Dove; stay right here with me, filling me with Your—" she suddenly stops. Champion! Where is he? She doesn't see him in his stall. She rushes over and finds him lying on his side.

"Champion, Champion, what is wrong with you?" She looks around and spots her backpack on the bench where she had accidentally left it last night. She sees that it's been opened…and to her horror, she sees the cellophane bag with the "sugar cubes" is completely empty! Oh no! How…? Who…? What happened?!

Jenny flies to the back door of the house, screaming, and crying, "Uncle Bubba, come quickly! Please, I need help!"

Her uncle quickly ends his call, shoves his phone in his pocket, and bolts out the door. "What's happened, Sugar? What's wrong?" He gently takes ahold of her shoulders, and says gently, "Now, calm down, Jen, and tell me."

Through her sobs, Jenny tells him something terrible has happened to Champion. He quickly follows her to the barn and seeing the horse laying on the ground he immediately calls their vet.

"Last night when you went to see him, was he all

right then, Sugar? Did you notice anything?"

Jenny shakes her head and continues sobbing. "But I think I know what happened… I just don't know how; I don't know who…"

Uncle Bubba sits her down on the bench and tries once more to calm her down. "Just take a deep breath, Sugar, you're not making much sense. Now slow down and tell me what you're trying to say."

Just then one of the twins, Bobby, pokes his head in the barn doorway. His eyes are wide with tears filling them. "I didn't mean to give all the sugar cubes to him. I just wanted to give him a couple, so he would like me. But he really gobbled them up, so I gave all of them to him. I didn't mean to make him sick. I didn't mean to hurt him, I swear!" He breaks down and begins to wail and sob, his whole body shaking. Uncle Bubba pulls him into his big arms and begins to soothe him. Aunt Bunnie and Billie Jean also appear, hearing all the crying and commotion.

Jenny sighs deeply. The moment of truth has come. The story begins to tearfully spill out of her. The sleepover. The girls. How she wanted them to like her. Kerri's older brother, saying there they were "all set." The cellophane bags tied up with ribbons that Kerri had brought out. How all the girls were popping these "sugar cubes" into their mouths and acting so strangely. How she didn't have the courage to tell them she didn't want those things. How she made up a lie about eating too much and her stomach hurting. And telling them she would try them later, when she was alone, showing them that she put the cubes into her backpack. Oh, why did she even put them into her backpack?? She weeps bitterly. Why didn't she just leave the stupid things there, and tell those girls she wasn't interested, and just leave! Fresh tears pour out of her. "When I went to see Champion late last night before I went to bed, I must have left my backpack here in the barn. I was so tired. I didn't realize it, and I just went to bed. Bobby must have found them…and thought they were sugar cubes…"

Bobby stops sobbing and looks at Jenny. "Well, what are they then, Jenny? They look like sugar cubes." His big blue eyes are wet and red. "I'm sorry, I'm sorry!" he wails again.

Jenny pulls him to her, hugs him hard, and says, "It's not your fault, Bobby. It's my fault; I should never have put them in my backpack!"

Bobby looks over at Champion still lying on the ground, and he whispers, "Is he dead?"

Uncle Bubba looks over at Champion, sighs, and says, "Well, he's still breathing even though it's very shallow. But he sure doesn't look like he's in very good shape. Dr. Mike is on his way. I'm sure he can tell us more."

7
A Wing and a Prayer

Jenny crawls next to Champion, puts her arms around his neck, buries her head in his mane, and cries fresh tears. "Oh, Champion, my Champion! I can't lose you! I am so sorry, it's all my fault, it's all my fault," she agonizes. Little Pogo, hearing her cries, makes his way over to her, slips into the stall, lays next to her, and licks her tears. She hugs him and kisses his nose. "Oh, Pogo. You understand, don't you, Boy?"

Aunt Bunnie and Uncle Bubba exchange sad looks and shake their heads. Hearing the vet's truck on the gravel, Uncle Bubba runs out to the front of the house to talk to him, to fill him in on the whole sad mess. Aunt Bunnie kneels down beside Jenny, and cries with her. Jenny suddenly looks up into her aunt's eyes. "Maybe we could pray for Champion?" she whispers through her tears.

"Yes, Jenny, dear, we can certainly pray for him.

God is the God of all creation. Do you want to say a prayer for Champion?"

Jenny kneels next to her aunt, turns her eyes upward, and for the first time in her life, utters a prayer to a God she doesn't know and has held a grudge against, but hopes will hear her. She is desperate. "Dear God, it's me, Jenny, "she whispers. "I don't know why You took my mom and dad and brother. Maybe You just wanted them to live with You. I've been pretty mad at You for that." She stops, shakily sighs, and then continues. "This horse means everything to me. I'm so sorry for bringing those drugs home in my backpack. I will never do anything so dumb again, I promise. Please, please, please, God, don't let Champion die—I love him so much!"

She throws herself on her horse once more and buries her tearstained face on his neck. Aunt Bunnie also looks upward with tears rolling down her cheeks, and breathes, "Please, God, please."

The vet comes in to examine Champion, running his hands over him, checking his eyes, his mouth, and listening to his heart. He shakes his head. "Well, I've never had a case like this," he starts. "I'll need to try to get some charcoal mixed with water down him, in a tube. I've done that in cases of horses ingesting plant poisons. But I don't know. Seems like what was in those cubes was a pretty potent drug." He glances at Jenny who hangs her head. "I'll be honest. I'd be surprised if he even makes it through the night. His heartbeat is very slow, and I don't like his shallow breathing, or how his eyes look. Such a shame, such a beautiful horse. I don't know if you're praying people, but frankly, it's going to take a miracle, folks."

The vet quickly opens his bag and runs a tube with the charcoal mixture into the unmoving horse's mouth. He shakes his head again, and as he walks away, he tells Jenny's uncle, "Call me if there's any…change." Bubba looks down and nods sadly.

Jenny doesn't leave Champion's side for the rest of the day, and all through the night. She hardly eats anything off the tray of food her aunt brings out to her. Pogo joins her in the vigil, never leaving her side. Her aunt and uncle are really getting worried about her. "What are we going to do, Bunnie? You know how much that horse means to her. You heard what the vet said. That horse hasn't got a wing and a prayer to survive. It will kill her…especially after all that sweet thing's been through. What a journey she's been on. Oh, Lordy, Lordy," Bubba breaths, putting his hands over his face.

Aunt Bunnie pulls her husband's hands away from his face, looks him in the eye, and says, "Now listen here, Bubba. We are not throwin' in the towel yet. That little girl out there actually prayed for the first time in her life. We are not going to give up hope. We are going to keep on prayin' and hopin'. Period. But in the meantime, I've got a phone call to make to a certain young lady's Mama, who, I'm sure, doesn't know what she's been up to."

The call to Kerri's mother, Doris, isn't easy for Bunnie, but the lady has to know the truth about what her daughter and son are involved in. Bunnie shares the whole story with her, and Doris is shocked but grateful that Bunnie has been completely honest with her.

"To tell you the truth, I haven't been paying much attention to what my kids have been doing," she tells Bunnie tearfully. "Ever since my Joe ran off with that…that… young woman, I've been a mess. I just don't know how he could do this to me, to his kids," she says bitterly. "I guess I've just been trying to make it through the day. I know my son has been real angry, and it's been easier around the house when he's not here—which seems to be a lot more lately. I've just been letting Kerri have her parties. I think she's been real depressed. She misses her daddy. Oh, Bunnie, I'm so sorry about all of this. I know your Jenny has been through so much already, losing her parents and all—which is why I wanted Kerri to invite her over. Oh, Lord, I hope she doesn't lose her pony. That would be a cryin' shame."

Bunnie listens patiently, with a sympathetic ear. "Yes, the vet didn't give us a sliver of hope, but we're all still praying. But back to your troubles, Doris, I know a very good family counselor. Do y'all want his number?"

"Oh, yes, Bunnie, I would really appreciate that. We need all the help we can get as a family. None of us have been coping very well, you know. I've been drinking a lot more…and my kids…well, now I know what they've been up to. Oh, Lord, how could I let this happen?" And she begins to cry again, softly.

Bunnie waits a minute, then gently says, "Oh, hon, I'm so sorry. I know you're having a hard time. You know, we've got a prayer group that meets on Friday nights, real nice folks. No one puts on airs, just real down to earth. Everybody's got problems. You'd be most welcomed to join us."

Doris thanks Bunnie, says she'll think about it, and sure appreciates the invitation. Bunnie sighs as she hangs up the phone, and just shakes her head. She thinks about Doris' husband leaving her like that, causing so much pain. Such a shame. No wonder she and her kids are messed up. They are all hurting. She hopes they'll all get the help they need. Meanwhile, she makes her way outside to the barn. Needs to check on her girl.

8
Mysterious Ways

Jenny's vigil has gone on all day, all night, and now the following day. She has not left Champion's side and Pogo hasn't left her side. As her eyelids droop from not having slept all night, exhausted and spent, she suddenly feels some movement beneath her. Champion is stirring! He gets up on one knee, sees Jenny, and nickers. It looks to Jenny as though he's trying to stand up! She jumps up, and watches, stunned, as Champion struggles a minute, then finally gets up to a standing position, and noses Jenny gently. Then he whinnies loudly and heads for his feeding bin. Jenny throws her arms around his neck, hugs him, and cries tears of joy! "Oh, Champion! I can't believe it, you're okay! Oh, my beautiful, beautiful, Champion!" Turning her eyes to heaven she cries, "Thank You, thank You, thank You! You heard me! You are real! You do care!"

Pogo's tail starts wagging, and he jumps up and

down, just like a pogo stick, and cries out little joyful barks. Aunt Bunnie reaches the barn by then, and she just can't believe her eyes. Her hand flies to her mouth, and all she can say is, "Oh, my Lord..."

News travels fast in a small town, and this news of the horse's miraculous recovery spreads lightning fast. Many friends and neighbors come by to tell Jenny how happy they are for her and Champion, and to see for themselves this walking, prancing, galloping miracle.

One day a truck pulls up in front of the house, and a young girl gets out on the passenger side. It is the shy girl, Anna, the one from Jenny's school, the only one who has ever truly been kind to her. This is the first time she has been to Jenny's home. Jenny spots her, waves from the barn, and calls out, "Anna! I'm over here!"

Anna shyly walks over. "I heard all about your horse. Jenny, is it really true? Was he brought back from the dead?"

Jenny laughs. "Well, that's a bit of an exaggeration, but yeah, no one thought he was going to make it. I'll tell you the whole story. Want to chill in my room? Can you hang out? Want to stay for dinner? I'm sure my aunt and uncle won't mind."

Anna smiles. "Sure, I'll just go ask my dad to pick me up later, ok?"

Aunt Bunnie watches the girls from the kitchen

window and smiles. She whispers, "You do work in mysterious ways, don't You?"

"What was that, Bunnie Honey?" asks Uncle Bubba, who is reading his paper.

"Oh, nothing, Hon. Just saying I better set another plate. Looks like Jenny's friend might stay for dinner." Their eyes meet, and they both smile.

"This whole thing is really somethin', isn't it, Bun? I hear the newspapers want to write up a story about it. Imagine that. Well, why not? It'd be nice for folks to read about some good news for a change, wouldn't it?"

Bunnie smiles again. "Yes, it would. It sure would."

In the days ahead as Champion canters down the dirt road, with Jenny astride his strong back, friends and neighbors can clearly hear her voice ringing out, singing a sweet song. They also hear her cry, "Oh, my sweet Champion, well done! You're even finer than the great Pegasus! Now take flight!" And their hearts swell. They smile and wave to her. For the first time, they don't even notice her New York accent. What they hear is the sound of joy, the sound of healing, the sound of hope, and the sound of the answer to a young girl's prayer.

Discussion Questions

1) When our story opens we discover that Jenny is now living in a different place with a different family. Why is that?

2) What are some of the challenges Jenny faces in this new situation?

3) Why is her birthday especially difficult for her? What is a trigger?

4) What makes Jenny's birthday gift extra special to her?

5) What are some of the challenges Jenny faces at school?

6) What is a positive coping strategy?

7) Name any of the positive coping strategies Jenny uses.

8) How does Jenny feel about going to the sleepover?

9) What does Jenny do to try to give the other girls the impression that she is not a loser? What would have been a better choice?

10) What are the consequences of her actions?

11) Whose fault is it that Champion almost dies? Jenny's, Bobby's, Kerri's, or Kerri's brother?

12) Name anything positive that happens, or any lessons that are learned, in spite of Jenny's poor choice.

The *Addiction Dragon* is destroying the lives of children in your neighborhood.

Stop the Addiction Dragon before your kids get hooked

WingMan Books
The best place for kids to learn about the pitfalls of addiction.

Always Fun - Never Preachy

Buy books at
breakfreestayfree.com

CPSIA information can be obtained
at www.ICGtesting.com
Printed in the USA
JSHW080515100223
37512JS00002B/101